You Can
Succeed Beyond
SCHOOL
&
WORK

Leveraging The Power Of Visionary Living

FEMI ADUN
Author of Unlock Your Future

DEDICATION

I dedicate this book to my cheerleader, my best friend, and wife, Busola Adun. You have helped me to succeed. I love you deeply.

CONTENTS

PREFACE

God, the creator, created you and me for a purpose, a reason greater than you can imagine, more significant than the four walls of the school or the beauty of any office space. Life is more than these two; going to school and getting a job. Although these two factors can contribute to your success in life, however, they have limitations.

Real success in life outweighs getting a degree and securing a good job; it is beyond your imagination. Your educational certifications or the top management position you will occupy will not put you in the class of men and women of a great legacy. The world today has in it people who have outstanding qualifications or occupy a position at senior management levels living unfulfilled lives or that have died mysteriously, uncelebrated, and some sadly unannounced. If you wonder why the world is full of such people, it is either because they failed to discover their purpose or failed to fulfill the very reason they were born.

You truly begin to experience real success when you start living for the purpose God created you because it takes you far beyond education or career success, far beyond it. The primary reasons most people don't fulfill the purpose for which they exist is either because they are ignorant of it and, of course, what you don't know, you can't pursue, neither can you achieve or afraid to let go of their immediate comfort. No one can reach for his or her purpose for existing except it has been disclosed. The revelation of your purpose is called vision. Without a God-given vision, you can limit the personal success you can attain in life, but the peaks are limitless with knowledge of it.

Friend, this book is not another book to talk about vision but a practical guide to knowing what vision is, having it, and realizing it. Get ready to undertake your transformation for the topmost.

See you at the top.

09

one

There is a place meant for you, a level you must attain. The purpose of going to school is not to end up in a job; it is only a pathway to fulfilling the purpose for which you exist. Vision is the only thing that reveals to a man his destination in life.

Chapter 1

VISION

"I knew you before you were formed in your mother's womb before you were given birth to I ordained you be a prophet" Jeremiah 1:5

WHAT IS VISION?

Without an accurate and adequate purpose of anything, its utilization will be unachievable; it can even lead to mismanagement, and mismanaging one's life is the most significant self-harm. In this chapter, I will like to share some definitions of what vision is with you to enable you to have a better understanding of why you are here on earth. An important question you should seek to answer is not one of the school examinations or your boss at work, but the critical question of "Why you are here on earth."

VISION IS A DIVINE REVELATION OF YOUR PURPOSE

No one can determine why they want to be here on earth; you can only discover it through revelation. According to the Bible, which is God's word, in Jeremiah 1:5, God said to a young man called Jeremiah.

> *"Before I shaped you in the womb, I knew all about you. Before you saw the light of day, I had holy plans for you: A prophet to the nations — that's what I had in mind for you." (MSG)*

Here was God revealing to Jeremiah his purpose for existing, like He did with Moses (read Exodus chapter 3) and several other bible characters who, from generation to generation, many including me, have continued to learn and teach success principles from their legacies.

You are for a purpose, and the pursuit of it will lead you to a rich and fulfilling life. Like every product has its functions determined by its manufacturer, so is your assignment determined by God. The Bible says we are God's workmanship (work) created for a purpose, which is good (***See Ephesians 2:10***). You are born for a unique purpose, but you need to know what purpose you have been born before you can achieve it.

VISION IS A PICTURE OF GOD'S AGENDA FOR YOUR FUTURE

There is a program arranged by God to fulfill our destiny but imagine if there were no event schedules, the result would be catastrophic; this explains why many are in a rat race. Without a visible plan, there can't be order in an event, more so in your life. Imagine a lecture delivered before students arrive in the classroom, or a sermon is preached in church before the congregation gets to the meeting. It will be totally out of place and ridiculous; such is a life without a purpose. You need to know what God wants you to do in an order and manner in which He reveals it to you. Jeremiah also received a detailed revelation of what he was pre-ordained to do according to the book of Jeremiah 1;

> *"**God reached out, touched my mouth, and said, "Look! I've just put my words in your mouth — hand-delivered! See what I've done? I've given you a job to do among nations and governments—a red-letter day! Your job is to pull up and tear down, take apart and demolish, And then start over building and planting."** (Jeremiah1:10, MSG).*

You will notice that God revealed Jeremiah's purpose to him in explicit detail. Just as his vision's fulfillment came in stages, you also need an agenda - GOD'S AGENDA for your life to create a balanced life.

VISION IS THE REVEALED KNOWLEDGE OF YOUR PREDESTINATION.

There is rarely anyone asked about their destination, who says "I don't know" except for a mentally incapacitated individual. God has never been an author of confusion, and He will never be; even when He told Abraham to leave his home, God said, "... to a land I will show you" (Genesis 12:1, Acts 7:3), so everyone has a destination in life.

There is a place meant for you, a level you must attain. The purpose of going to school is not to end up in a job; it is only a pathway to fulfilling the purpose for which you exist. Vision is the only thing that reveals to a man his destination in life. Every race in life has a goal, including the rat race. It would either be running to the cheese or its hideout. So in the real sense of it, no one is living without a destiny.

If your life indeed has a meaningful end, then it must begin with a sense of destiny. It is paramount to wake up every day doing whatever it is you do, knowing it's all an effort to keep you in line and get you closer to your life destination. Settling for less is easy when you don't know where you are heading to in life, ministry, business, or in your career. God has never started anyone in his or her life race without giving a sense of destiny as a guiding factor in pursuing purpose. When God chose Paul for apostleship, as documented in Acts 9, God made sure Paul had an idea of what lies ahead of him.

But the Master said, "Don't argue. Go! I have picked him as my representative to non-Jews and kings and Jews. And now I'm about to show him what he's in for—the hard suffering that goes with this job." - Acts 9:15-16 (MSG)

Now you see, it is not God's way keeping you in the dark to figure out why you are here on earth. Most times, Christians keep themselves ignorant of their predestination either because they choose to live life without God or in disobedience to His directions. If you are reading this book, do not attempt any of these two!

Apart from the benefit of knowledge, I have decided to start this book, defining what vision is to help you know some of its purposes, which I will share in the next chapter. There is a purpose to every bit of knowledge we acquire and retain. Experience without its purpose is useless and not beneficial. We would talk more about the purpose of vision in the next chapter.

two

> *A person who lacks vision cannot see beyond the present state of things and, of course, will most likely gamble through his/her entire life. I can tell you for sure that's not the life God intended for man.*

Chapter 2

PURPOSE OF VISION

▼

"If people can't see what God is doing, they stumble all over themselves; But when they attend to what he reveals, they are most blessed." Proverb 29:18 - MSG

There several things having a vision does for you, which makes your life as visionary exquisite. Hardly is there a man or woman who is truly a visionary whose life ends like every other individual. Living a life of vision will certainly place several demands on you but eventually will substantially transform your life for the best. This conclusion is not based on some flimsy ideology but from my personal experience. I have studied the many biographies of the men and women who have revolutionized contemporary thinking through visionary living. My life did not begin to change until I understood and submitted to the intense power of visionary living when I discovered three powerful forces of vision. Now, let us explore three of these vital purposes of vision.

REFINES
- Vision Refines You

The first thing a vision does in anyone's life is to refine the visionary. It brings out the most authentic version of you and not the person your environment or circumstances have subjected you to. The first thing Jeremiah addressed when he received his vision from the Lord was his circumstances; he said

> *"But I said, "Hold it, Master God! Look at me. I don't know anything. I'm only a boy!" (Jeremiah 1:6 MSG).*

In truth, there was nothing wrong with what Jeremiah said; it only accentuates that a divine revelation of what God designed you to do will challenge your current capabilities. An infant prince or princess will have gone through all the messing ups and falling downs to become the king or queen eventually. However, through this period, their status as a prince or princess does not change, for he or she will someday become the king or queen. All of these are just temporary conditions that can't change him or her from what they were born to be - a king or queen!

A real VISION does not speak the same language as the poverty from the family background or what people say about you, not even the harshness of the economic status of the nation you are either born in or that you reside. None-withstanding!

What vision does is to bring out your status as a king, but condition says you must pass through teething stages as a baby prince, like all gold, must go through refinery to achieve its majestic elegance.

According to Sam Adeyemi, Vision gives an individual the ability to see people and places the way they could be and not how they appear. This statement is a powerful statement that often time, too many people are quick to judge a book by its cover and too quickly reach a conclusion; it's of no benefit to them. This attitude is why many individuals, corporations, and even nations haven't experienced possible reformation due to a lack of visionary thinking and living. A person who lacks vision cannot see beyond the present state of things and, of course, will most likely gamble through his/her entire life. I can tell you for sure that's not the life God intended for man.

Isaiah, chosen by God a prophet, wasn't that much of a good communicator. However, according to him, God refined him in writing how the Lord touched his tongue with a coal of fire, leading to his powerful communication skill. Why? Isaiah was purposed by God to be a spokesman to the nations, but Isaiah, in his unrefined state, did not possess the capacity required to fulfill this assignment.

The Bible also recorded one of the Bible patriarchs, Moses, a stammerer before he received his vision from the Lord, and by the time God has finished working on Moses, he had become a great orator. A real Vision will bring out the best in you.

I have not always been who I am now; an autodidact, author, international speaker, business owner, mentor, coach, adviser, and consultant. As I mentioned in my book (*The Seed - principles of fruitfulness*), I was once a school dropout, which meant that not so much was expected of me, particularly within my social construct. However, my story is different now. Today I get messages from around the world telling how much of an inspiration I am. This is what the discovery of one's purpose in life does; it allows for personal transformation. You, too, can experience it!

CONFINES
- Vision Confines You

In addition to being refined, what vision does for you is to confine you; in other words, vision defines your boundaries. Anything you do in life that has no boundaries or limitations is dangerous for you. It is vital to understand your scope and appreciate that you a jack of all trade as a visionary. A key component for a visionary living is a keen focus and undivided energy. Every true visionary will tell you that you would have to live within certain boundaries to be successful at being a visionary, depending on your purpose. In my years of study, I have come across stories of men and women who failed to pursue a goal because they allow so many things to interfere with their God-given assignment. In the book of Jeremiah, God said to Jeremiah.

"Don't say, 'I'm only a boy.' I'll tell you where to go, and you'll go there. I'll let you know what to say, and you'll say it. Don't be afraid of a soul. I'll be right there, looking after you." God's Decree." (Jeremiah 1:7 MSG)

In other words, God was saying to Jeremiah as you and I, "you are not to do everything." God did not design you for every and anything; He created you for just one purpose. According to the Bible, Apostle Paul was a man committed to his vision said that all things are lawful for him, but not all things are helpful and edifying, meaning with a vision for one's life, not everything that seems good is right for you.

More than ever, I am very quick to say no nowadays to avoid unnecessary distractions and detour from my God-given purpose. It's challenging but beneficial in the long run for everyone in pursuit of a fulfilled vision.

Sometimes, when I'm driving home, I see several streets more beautiful than mine; still, I don't decide to go into these streets because none of it will lead me to my destination, and in this discussion, home is the vision.

A visionary places more excellent value on the essentials and everything can't be necessary. With a passion and desire to see as many people saved, Jesus Christ would have loved to preach to every single soul, but there were places He did not go. As a speaker, I have had to learn over the years that I can't be at every meeting in as much as public speaking is my passion.

If you are not ready to be disciplined, then be willing to accept failure.

On several occasions, Jesus Christ was asked to do things but disciplined enough to refuse as He understood that every vision has time boundaries. When you receive a vision from God, some people would have to stop being your friends, and you might have to stop visiting certain places; otherwise, you may never realize your vision.

Today, so many youths are pursuing degrees that have nothing to do with their God-designed purpose in life because they lack the knowledge of it. How would they then know what not to do? Thus, loads of frustrated undergraduates. Why then, should there not be cultism, rape, robbery, knife crimes, and all kinds of waywardness on the campuses and our streets? It is because vision, leadership, and character development are not a subject taught in most schools. When the purpose of life is not a part of the school curriculum, then the result of this is employees at the slightest opportunity will get involved in fraudulent activities at the workplace or non-engagement. Merely because they went through school frustrated, studying career courses, they did not derive any fulfillment from and yet forced to learn due to parental or environmental pressures. Even now, many young men and women are victims, frustrated because they are still living in the ignorance of the purpose for which they exist.

Over the years, I have advocated that young people should first discover the purpose they were born before going to school to study as education is to help an individual nurture his/her nature. I have found that school education enhances your mental faculties and abilities to help you maximize and fulfill your God-given purpose, not determine it. Doing this will help produce more graduates from various institutions with the mentality of creating their businesses or becoming business partners with existing companies, primarily in developing countries with a declining employment rate. By God's plan, everyone is destined to lead when living in purpose; it is when you out of purpose that you become a slave to others. My Bible tells me that you and I have been made kings to reign on earth (See the book of Revelation 5:10).

Friend, you must know why you exist to understand what not to do, who not to be with, and where not to go.

DEFINES
- Vision Defines You

Finally, in this chapter, in addition to vision refining and confining you, vision will also define you, which means your true identity is no longer guesswork. It states precisely who you are, what you are to do, and where you are designated. Self-definition is the first step towards distinction, and this determines the value you bring to the table. In the world we live in today, where the culture of trends and styles is fast shaping our way of life, it is becoming a massive challenge for this present generation to find their true identity. The rate of people trying to look like another person is unbelievable. You can't be mistaken for another person when you live for your vision. The content of God's plan and purpose for Jeremiah revealed his distinction.

> *"Before I shaped you in the womb, I knew all about you. Before you saw the light of day, I had holy plans for you: A prophet to the nations" that's what I had in mind for you." (Jeremiah, 1:5).*

A God-ordained vision to an individual is a revelation with a clear definition of purpose. Anyone who claims to have a picture and cannot define the vision in a statement or at least a sentence may be assuming one. A real vision must reveal something definite; a cause of/for action. Otherwise, the visionary will lack an identity or personality. One of the difficulties of the times you and I live in is that people, especially the youth, are getting into all sorts of negativity, which is mostly traceable to lack of identity. It is true that when an individual doesn't stand for something significant, they will eventually fall for everything irrelevant.

History records the life of Nelson Mandela, a true African patriot, and an exceptional leader. He refused to be defined by pain, hatred, and violence but by a vision of hope, love, and unity for his country South Africa. It would have been difficult or impossible for Mandela without a conceived vision for these sorts of national values to define his values along with these sets of qualities.

God is the one who created you, and when He gives you a vision, it means you then now have to find life meaning based on His plan for your life. It is also essential for you to know that His plan for your life will also determine your location per time. History is a record of events that took place somewhere in the world to fulfill your purpose in life.

Let me also mention that you are just not wired for everything. God created you for something that will guarantee your exploits and fulfillment in life and not only your portfolio of certificates or your well-put-together curriculum vitae (resumé) of job experiences.

There is an account in the Bible of some men who became disciples of Jesus Christ in spreading the good news at the expense of their career ambitions. Initially, everyone thought these young men had lost their minds to leave a lucrative business to preach all over towns, villages, and cities. However, these people didn't know that these folks had a call of God on their lives. Before anyone of them was born, God had a plan for them, and without the pursuit of this life-purpose, their lives will eventually have no real meaning. In my experience of pastoring and ministering to people worldwide, I have had the privilege of speaking with several people who admitted this truth. I have discovered that many people, irrespective of their caliber, become unfulfilled doing everything else other than the very purpose they were born after some time.

One time, a lady was invited to our church by a member of our worship services. As my custom is to meet every first-time guest at the end of the service, I met with this lady who told me during our brief conversation that she worked for the local authority with relatively good pay but wasn't finding fulfillment. In her words, she said, "Pastor, I feel there is more to me than what I am doing at my place of work at the moment." That! Right there is what I call a conflict between ambition and purpose.

I recently read an article by *Bratasanu (2016)*, a contributor to HuffPost, a American news and opinion website. He stated that 900 million people in 142 countries are dissatisfied with what they do in life. He further says that about 70 percent of the U.S. working class are unhappy and do not care for what they do in their jobs. In comparison, the millennials are the most dissatisfied and the least labor force that cares about what they do at work.

The solution to this will be that people, especially millennials, begin to intentionally embrace and pursue their God-given purpose. The only thing that brings surpassing success and true fulfillment to you or anyone is to do what others cannot do, and that is to fulfill your God-given purpose.

No one can do what God has designed for you, only you can, and that is what defines and stands you out. You ought not to be called by your name alone but also by your vision statement – YOUR LIFE PURPOSE. In the Bible, some folks were sent to John the Baptist to ask who he was, and in unambiguous terms, he said: "I am the voice of one crying out in the wilderness: make straight the way of the Lord." John is someone who knows what he is all about, not just what others call him.

If you are known only by your name, you cannot be greater than your certificate or job. In the text above, John the Baptist did not say "I am John Zacharias"; he defined himself by his life purpose. I do not want to be known just by my name. Like John, I want to be known for my God-given purpose.

Let me conclude this chapter with a saying of a superb friend of mine "when you allow vision to define, confine, and refine you; in the end, it makes you fine."

Purpose Of Vision

three

> *The things you can do with God influencing your life through His supernatural abilities are beyond our academic qualification and employee benefits. There is a way a vision from God or a revelation from His word can radically influence your thought processes enabling your mental capacity beyond the development of one's cognitive abilities or intelligent quotient academic information.*

3 INDISPENSABLE BENEFITS OF VISION

▼

"Blessed be the Lord, who daily loads us with benefits the God of our salvation" Psalm 68:19

3 INDISPENSABLE BENEFITS OF VISION

Everything that has a purpose must have benefits to it. I think that whatever will place a demand on you, your time and resources must be to your advantage or service to you in some ways. It is crucial that you carefully read through this chapter. If you have heard the saying that when the purpose of something is not known, then abuse is inevitable. Likewise, when the benefit of a thing is not known, under-utilization is unavoidable.

Now, let us explore some of the benefits of visionary living, and these are in no particular order.

IT'S SECURES DIVINE BACKING

The first benefit of having a God-given vision is that It secures for you God's backing. Any product that has no endorsement from its manufacturer may not have a real market value. The same is life without divine support. What is divine backing? It is God making His supernatural ability through His wisdom and grace available to you and me for the accomplishment of His purpose for each of us. Like every father will back his child, especially when he or she is doing what pleases him. Likewise, God can help you in significant ways when you, as His creation, commit to His master plan for your life.

The visible manifestations of God's backing in an individual's life are unfathomable; it is far beyond the human mind. In Exodus 3:12, God said to Moses, "I will certainly be with you," having received a vision from the God, and for this reason, Moses succeeded in rescuing the Israelite from the captivity and cruelty of the Egyptian ruler; something that seemed impossible for a single man. The things you can do with God influencing your life through His supernatural abilities are beyond our academic qualification and employee benefits. There is a way a vision from God or a revelation from His word can radically influence your thought processes enabling your mental capacity beyond the development of one's cognitive abilities or intelligent quotient academic information.

In Jeremiah 1, once the young Prophet was clear about his God-designed purpose, God also said to Jeremiah, "Do not be afraid for I will be with you," meaning that you can rely on God when you are in pursuit of His of purpose for you. As a student already living by purpose, you have an advantage over others to stay on track and avoid wasting time, energy, and resources other students who have no clue about purpose fall into, either in their academics, relationships, or personal life.

When God is for you, no one can be against you". So why do you have to go through life frustrated like so many individuals today? A life without the involvement of God will most likely end up a miserable one. When God is involved in a person's life challenges, it will still turn out to be a life of meaningful impact and dignity.

David, a shepherd boy, became king over Israel because God was with him. Moses, a fugitive, saved Israel from 400 years of bondage and parted the red sea because God was with him. Abraham became the father of many nations at 100 years old because God was with him. Sarah gave birth at a timeworn age because God was with her. A virgin gave birth because God was with her, yes! I once dropout out of school, but today through God's grace and wisdom has written several life-changing books, spoken to thousands of people worldwide – 25 nations so far, and trained several top management personnel in different sectors my leadership development programs.

These lives, including mine, are evidence of God's wisdom and power by ordinary people through visionary living, not necessarily because of an academic distinction or a senior management position.

Some other exceptional men and women have made history with an excellent account of incredible feats with God's help. The late Oral Roberts built an institution, Oral Roberts University, whose glory has lasted for many years. It is still very much recognized today for its products of purpose-driven individuals.

Billy Graham was another man who spoke to millions of people from various parts of the world and their government officials, ranging from presidents to business leaders. Academically speaking, this will require a lot to accomplish if possible.

These men were able to do great exploits being influenced by God because they lived a life of vision. They understood their purpose and gave their best, fulfilling it.

IT ATTRACTS DIVINE SUPPLY

Divine supply just means provision for the fulfillment of the vision. If you look at the word provision, you will notice it is a combination of two words, PRO and VISION, and PRO mean FOR while VISION means YOUR GOD-GIVEN ASSIGNMENT. The provision indicates the supply of resources FOR the fulfillment of your PURPOSE in LIFE, WHICH IS YOUR VISION.

It will be inconsistent with the character of God, for Him to hold a vision for you then withhold the necessary resources required for its accomplishment. Jeremiah said, ***"God is it not you who created me to be a prophet and how can I be a prophet when I don't have words to speak***," meaning that the fulfillment of my assignment as a prophet depends on the 'word resource' available to me. The Bible then records that "*God put forth His words in Jeremiah's mouth*," providing resources in the form of words for him, which led to the fulfillment of his Vision (Jeremiah chapter one verse nine).

God will always supply resources as long as your vision is from Him. It is true because I have experienced it several times on many occasions, and more so, His word from Philippians 4:19 is that "*He will supply all our need according to His riches in glory*." Divine supply comes in different forms; some come in human form. You will need human resources to fulfill your God-given assignment. I learned quite early in leadership that I am only as successful as people's quality. The earthly ministry Jesus Christ much depended on intensive human capital resources and still does today.

So many visionaries don't enjoy divine supply because they failed to look up to God for resources. They have turned divine supply to individual supply. They run after men for help, not God; it is only with God that all things are possible, not with mere mortals. The surest person to run to for academic challenges or career difficulties is God, not any human being who may end up taking advantage of you, or someone who will turn your life upside-down when you are having problems with your career.

I still remember trying to publish my first book in 2005. I had nothing, not a dime, to get my manuscript published and printed, but I continued to write and to celebrate its fulfillment. I was confident that God would supply; after all, He inspired me to write. The book 'THE SEED' was published, printed, and read in many nations worldwide. Glory and honor be to God for His supplies!

I encourage you to run with your God-given Vision and watch God blow your mind as He supernaturally provides for the accomplishment of what He's called you to do.

IT ENSURES THE REALITY OF YOUR PURSUIT

It is not everyone a racetrack that makes it to the finish line in the first position. Likewise, not everybody on the journey of life comes out fulfilled with a sense of accomplishment. However, it is different for those who live their lives to pursue their God-given Vision because the destination is unique to every individual.

The very moment Jeremiah received a clear vision of his purpose, hear what God said to him, "***You have seen well, for I am ready to perform*** My word." There is a performance for every vision God gives; I have not seen a pursued vision from God that does not end up in reality. Everything God settled in the spiritual realm ended up in the physical, so why would God create you for great things and not perform it on earth if you dare to pursue it.

Prophet Jeremiah had already been a prophet in the spirit realm before conception in his mother's womb, not when he was in the womb or after delivery was he a prophet. In Jeremiah's book, God said chapter one, verse five that He knew him, sanctified and ordained him to be a Prophet to the Nations. Now the question is, did Jeremiah become a prophet when he was eventually born into this world? Of course, he did, and that is why today he is referred to as Prophet Jeremiah.

Before my birth, God told my mother some specific things concerning me: I would live to serve my generation through the ministry gifts deposited in me by God with undeniable proof but guess what? It didn't turn out to be like that for the first twenty-two years of my life, not at all. I was very far from it; I did not look like a man God would ever want to use to display His greatness. I was terrible, doing all sorts of things ranging from theft to smoking and many other harmful habits, which eventually led to dropping out of school.

Today the story has changed; I am a brand-new person, living the life prophesied to my late mother, which she continually spoke to me even when the situation remained so bad, and far from what God promised her.

I remember those words of my precious mother distinctly. She will say to me during those dark times when I came home drunk each night, "Son, this is not God's plan for you, this is just what the devil wants to make out of you. I believe God's purpose for your life will come to pass". Eventually, I had an encounter that changed my life, which set me on the path God had predestined for me, and everything began to change positively until this present moment.

Aligning with God's plan for your life is the only way to live an extraordinary and fulfilling life. Jesus said to His disciples, "Follow me, and I will make you fishers of men." It meant that there was more to them at the time. He met them, and they needed to align with destiny.

Friend, if you are already nurturing your God-given vision, do not stop even if it seems more significant than you. A big vision is a reason you need the help of God. I pray that you receive divine assistance in realizing your dream in Jesus' name, Amen!

3 Indispensable Benefits of Vision

four

▼

> *Not every person that receives a vision fulfills it, due to the negligence of responsibility. To walk in the fulfillment of a vision requires dedication and commitment to work; otherwise, God can't do much no matter the size of the vision.*

Chapter 4

DYNAMICS OF VISION

▼

"For which of you intending to build a tower, does not sit down first and count the cost whether he has enough to finish it" Luke 14:28

It is essential to accept that your God-given Vision will not fulfill itself. Every vision that will become a reality requires your active participation. It is impossible to place total responsibility on God for the fulfillment of your vision. God has His part, and we also have our role in fulfilling His divine purpose for our lives. The good thing is that God is always ready to play His part, but we are still the problem; many individuals find it challenging to be responsible, even for their lives.

There is something everyone must do to get the ball rolling, and that is kicking it. Any ball not kicked will never be scored. Therefore, responsibility is on whoever wants to kick the ball into the goal net and the same fault lies with you and me. There is a tremendous responsibility required from any visionary to see their God-given Vision come to pass.

Not every person that receives a vision fulfills it, due to the negligence of responsibility. To walk in the fulfillment of a vision requires dedication and commitment to work; otherwise, God can't do much no matter the size of the vision.

I learned from one of my mentors that all promises from God to humanity come with some conditions. Not until these conditions are met; God will not commit to its reality. He further stated that, when these conditions are satisfied, the promise graduates into a covenant, which commits God to its fulfillment. You and I must take responsibility in life. Without it, we'll never reach our full potential. Haven't you heard that everything valuable has a price, for it to be total obtainable price must be paid?

In this book, vision dynamics consist of eight steps divided into two stages that you and I must take to attain fulfillment. The first stage of the vision dynamics teaches us how to have a vision while the second phase will take us through practical steps in turning our vision into reality.

Get set! As we make an exploration together in discovering what makes an individual succeed beyond school and work!

Dynamics of Vision

five

> *Relationship with God is more than a commitment to God; it's a connection with God via His word (studying to imbibe it), prayer, and fasting. These three connecting factors go beyond the church affair; it's a personal affair.*

Chapter 5

STAGE ONE DYNAMICS OF VISION: HOW TO DISCOVER YOU GOD-GIVEN VISION

▼

"I will stand my watch and set myself on the tower, and watch to see what the Lord will say to me." - Habakkuk 2:1

As mentioned in the previous pages of this book, you are not here on earth to determine why you are here; you are here to discover your purpose. A God-given vision is not an ambition; therefore, you can't create a vision for yourself; you can only find God's pre-plan for your existence.

The question now is, how can you receive anything from someone without relating to that individual? It will be difficult for you to receive anything from me if we do not have an existing relationship. So, the first step in this stage is;

STEP 1 - RELATION

I did a study on the word "relation," and I discovered it means "a meaningful connection or association between two or more things, e.g., one based on the similarity or relevance of one thing to another."

Through a connection to God, a revelation of your assignment here on earth is disclosed. In Habakkuk, chapter 2: 1, prophet Habakkuk received his Vision from God. He said,

> ***"I will stand my watch and set myself on a tower, and watch what God will say to me, and what I will answer when I am corrected" and in verse two of the same chapter, he continued, "Then the Lord answered me and said: "Write the vision and make it plain on tablets, that he may run who reads it."***

From the record above, it is apparent that there was a relationship between him and God before a vision. The Prophet said he would stand on a tower, meaning that he will separate himself onto God. Today Christians still do this. You will hear statements like, "I am going to the mountain to pray." There is nothing wrong with this practice if you have a mountain in the city or country where you live.

On many occasions, Jesus Christ went to the mountain to have a quiet time with His heavenly Father, so it's okay to find a secluded place to pray. It is really not about the mountain, but what you do or what happens there. Jesus went on the mountain whenever He wanted to spend time alone with God relating with Him, and each time He came back, He came down full of power to do more exploits. However, what we have around today are groups of people going to the mountain to waste their time. Some hills have even become a tourist attraction.

There is no way you can receive a revelation of your purpose in life without having a good connection with God. I don't mean just going to church (going to church is very important) but what I mean is this; is going to church be because you long to build a deeper relationship with God or other reasons best known to you? A relationship with God goes beyond your regular attendance in a church building or a journey to a mountain top.

Relationship with God is more than a commitment to God; it's a connection with God via His word (studying to imbibe it), prayer, and fasting. These three connecting factors go beyond the church affair; it's a personal affair.

In Matthew, chapter fifteen, Jesus Christ also pointed out this issue from verses seven to eight, talking about the scribes and Pharisees.

"hypocrites! Well, did Isaiah prophesy about you are saying: 'these people draw near to me with their mouth

and honor me with their lips, but their heart is far from me".

Connection supersedes commitment. Just like Martha was committed and Mary was connected (see the book of Luke 10:38-42). Some individuals go to church for public relations and not for a deeper connection with God. Such people only cause division in the house of God and distractions for others in the pursuit of their God-given assignment relating to them. As a parishioner, God must be the sole object of our worship and our purpose of attending a local church.

Matthew 6:22 states that "if your eye is single, your whole body will be full of light," which my understanding is a piece of critical advice to keep one's eye focus on God to attain fulfillment in life. Another mentor of mine once said, "you can't make one of your eyes look up while the other looks down at the same time." In other words, you cannot depend on God to receive a vision and also, at the same time, be relying on a man for the fulfillment of a God-given vision.

Before I conclude this note, allow me to share one other crucial factor in establishing a vital connection with God. Matthew, chapter five, verse eight, states, ***"Blessed are the pure in the heart, for they shall see God".*** Only a pure-hearted man, not just a hearted man, can receive a vision from God.

Friend, just if you realize you need to make a heart reconnection to God, why not decided to reconnect with Him right away. It will only take a short but heartfelt prayer.

Something like this or the way you best know:

"Lord Jesus, I am deciding to accept you into my life right now. Please cleanse me from any impurity hindering my connecting to You. I request this in Your name, Amen!

STEP 2 - CONCEPTION

Every baby born was first conceived, so must every vision be birthed. The same is an idea that you can't capture in your mind cannot be manufactured. Conception is the act of capturing a revelation from God, and without it, delivery is impossible. God will not reveal a vision to a man who cannot capture it because it is like pouring water into a basket. God doesn't waste His resources, which is why He does not just give visions without discretion.

Thank God for the comfort of the Holy Spirit. Still, it could be very frustrating for a man whose wife cannot conceive a child after several attempts, so it is with God when He wants to release to us a revelation of His plan, especially for our lives and don't conceive it. Your inability to conceive a vision limits God in your life.

Amos 3:7 says, Surely the Lord God does nothing without revealing His plan to His servants the Prophet. It explains why God said to the Children of Israel, "See! I have given the land to you", which means that their possession of the Promised Land lies in their ability to first CONCEIVE their victory against the existing occupants.

God's promises to you and me indeed are one of a glorious destiny, but that isn't a guarantee that you will have it without conceiving it. At this point, let me answer the question running through your mind; perhaps you are wondering how you will conceive it. Hebrews 11:1is the answer "faith is the substance of things hoped for and the evidence of things not seen." Every child of God can only conceive and obtain God's promises by faith because faith gives us the capacity to see beyond the immediate into God's ultimate plan for one's life.

You must see it because that is the only thing that gets God committed; seeing is your surety that you will have it. It is more than knowing what God has planned for you; it's believing it to the point that it becomes an imprint in your spirit. Several times, Jesus told His disciples to have faith, to believe all that He kept revealing to them as it relates to their future and what was possible in God.

In Proverb twenty-three verse seven, we are told that "As a man thinks in his heart, so is he." I learned that sometimes the Bible uses the heart in place of the mind. In other words, whatever finds its way into your mind will gain control over your life. Your mind plays an essential role in the conception of a vision from God.

Matthew 12:35says, "***A good man out of the good treasure of his heart brings forth good things, and an evil man brings forth evil things***."

Here is the word of God, and it is final. It says whatever is in your heart will out rightly determine your productivity in life. My pastor, Dr. Sam Adeyemi, often says, "ideas have wings, and they can fly away. Therefore, you and I must capture them quick". He taught me the principle of journaling, writing down the things God reveals to me.

The Prophet Habakkuk was told by God in Habakkuk chapter two, verse two, to write the vision given to him so that achieving it will be more comfortable as he sees it. Remember what you see, not once but continuously, is what sticks to your mind, which inevitably determines what you will become. Writing down your vision is a potent act of conception.

Every revelation is worth documenting; imagine if I had not written this revelation, how would it become a blessing to you or my generation and the generation to come? Make it a habit beginning now, to write down everything God says to you. I know even before you finish reading this book, God will reveal important truths to you. Get prepared!

STEP 3 - CONVICTION

Conviction is your strong belief in what you have been told by God concerning your destiny, even though it may seem impossible. The lack of conviction has hindered more people from maximizing their potentials and fulfilling their purpose in life. I called this the "belief system," It is vital because it is the bridge you will need to cross into the next stage, realizing your vision.

I once heard a large organization leader said he wasn't surprised at the level of global successes they had achieved; instead, he would have been surprised if they hadn't. According to him, God had revealed this to him many years ago, and he believed it.

In 2 Chronicles 20:20, the Bible says, ***"believe in the Lord your God, and you will be established..."***. Without you believing what God has said about your purpose, you can never become it on earth.

As an undergraduate, God tells you before you leave school to start your own company, and it will eventually become a world-class organization. Still, because no one has ever done anything significant in your family lineage, you allow doubt to gain control over your mind. Or you are an employee and the same is said to you; obviously, everybody knows you got into the job with a below-average degree, so you say to yourself it can't be possible. It is not true because the word of God does not say so; what it says is what it is "with God; all things are possible."

In the book of Mark, chapter nine and verse twenty-three, Jesus said, "***If you can believe, all things are possible to him who believes***." Did he say some things? No! He said, "all things" when you believe, whatever revelation you receive from God about your destiny, you are on your way to realizing it. No man in history did anything significant in life without a robust belief system that it was possible. I will forever talk about the great Rolihlahla Mandela, who believed in a course and gave his best to it, even though he had to pay a considerable price for it, but today his pain was not in vain, a great one indeed.

A songwriter said, "I believe I can fly; I believe I can touch the sky." Each time I think about these two powerful life-transforming proclamations, I think of ' The Wright Brothers'. People believed it impossible to create an object that flies, but the brothers invented the airplane because they believed. You will never go beyond your belief system in life.

One of the reasons your belief system is crucial is that God will not give you a vision according to your current size or capacity. He will give you a ten times greater vision than you are to keep you depending on him for its fulfillment.

Any Vision that exempts you from believing God is not a

vision from God. Every great man I have studied up to date. All have an audacity of faith. You will wonder how I come to this conclusion? Of course, through their results, they are evidence of men who walked with God, and before you can walk with God, you must first please Him. So how do you please God?

According to the word of God in Hebrews chapter eleven and verse six, "***But without Faith, it is impossible to please Him, for he who comes to God must believe that he is and that He is a rewarder of those who diligently seek Him***." The only thing that moves God towards any man with a vision is faith. I have read a lot of books about men and women who, by faith, did the impossible. This book you are reading is a product of faith in God.

My mentor said, "Faith partners you with God to do the impossible," without it, you are vulnerable to molestations of the enemy - the devil. But when your belief system is robust, you enter into an active partnership with God Himself, and the Bible says, with God, all things are possible.

six

> *Any vision that puts total responsibility on God is fake; you and I will always have a part to play in fulfilling our God-given Vision. No matter how heavenly it is, it will never be self-fulfilling.*

Chapter 6

STAGE TWO DYNAMICS OF VISION: HOW TO REALIZE YOUR VISION

▼

"Then the Lord answered me and said, Write the Vision and make it plain on a tablet that he may run who reads it, for the vision is yet for an appointed time; but in the end, it will speak, and it will not lie. Though it tarries, wait for it because it will surely come, it will not tarry" - Habakkuk 2:2-3

How to realize a God-given is where the line is drawn. As they say, "where the rubber meets the road." I call the application of faith, acting on what you believe. You will learn in this chapter, you have more responsibilities on you, and without a practical commitment to these responsibilities, you can never realize your God-given vision. Have you ever heard a statement like "there is no free lunch"? If you have not, then hear it now. There is a price to pay for greatness, and some of them are about to be revealed to you.

I once heard someone said, the fact you are a professor in Agriculture does not excuse you from practicing the principles of sowing and reaping. That you know how to plant and harvest Apples theoretically (by textbook) is not enough reason you will have apple trees just growing in your garden or farm. For that to happen, that individual must practically apply all the necessary principles on the field before he/she can grow an apple tree and, of course, have apples to eat. It means that the theoretical analysis on how to plant and harvest apples is enough to provide him apples; It is the practical commitment of his knowledge that gets the job done.

The truth is hard, but it delivers! No lazy man will ever fulfill his destiny because every great vision requires commitment. It is time to buckle up, as I take you through some steps I discovered to help realize your vision.

STEP 4: ACTION

In physics, one of the essential laws that govern life is the law of motion. A physicist, Isaac Newton, propounded this law; he stated the law of motion thus; "Every object remains at a state of rest until a force is applied." The same is the vision without action. According to the law of motion, your vision is like an object maintaining a standstill, and action is the force needed to set it in motion. Action is what sets your vision into motion; without it, your vision will remain unachievable.

In Habakkuk chapter two, verse two, God made it clear to Prophet Habakkuk that it was vital for him to write down his vision, and it was because writing it down will make it easier to run with it (take action). Any vision that does not get you running is not a vision; it's a dream; you should wake up.

If you must see the reality of your God-given vision, you must be ready to take practical steps, and here is a crucial one you cannot miss. I will agree with you if you say the Grace of God is available. Still, I also learned from Apostle Paul, from the book of first Corinthians chapter fifteen and verse ten who stated, "***By the grace of God I am what I am, and His grace toward me was not in vain, but I labored more abundantly than they all, yet not I, but the grace of God which was with me***."

Here was a man who was commissioned with the message of God's Grace still acknowledging labor, the diligent work he was required to do, to fulfill his assignment. Any vision that puts total responsibility on God is fake; you and I will always have a part to play in fulfilling our God-given Vision. No matter how heavenly it is, it will never be self-fulfilling.

After your connection with God has secured a heavenly vision for you and you have successfully captured it and then believing it is no more a struggle. The next thing for you to do is to begin to take practical steps one after the other in line with the fulfillment of your vision. I remember the process of writing and publishing my first book, I did not have any money, but I had a vital connection with God. I had the revelation of the book and, at the same time, a revelation of starting my own publishing company. Going by the second step in the first stage of the dynamics of fulfilling vision, I made a graphic design of the book cover and a label carrying on it the logo of my publishing company. So, I pinned it on the wall in my room, which represented a successful conception. So, what next?

I searched for an editor for the manuscript, and God supernaturally stepped in and supplied every other resource required for the successful completion of the project. Even till the launch, provisions kept coming in to meet the occasion's needs, including the national newspapers report about my newly released book. The truth is that, if you do not step out, God will not step in. Up to date, I still marvel at how my little effort resulted in something great. I sold my book in the United Kingdom, advertised all over Europe and the world at large via the internet, bookstores, and through other forms of media advert.

In Summary, this is what I learned from that experience.

Vision - action = Frustration but Vision + action = Realization.

Action sequentially follows after conviction because the Bible says "faith without works is dead" in other words, your vision without action leads to a dead vision, and a dead vision renders the visionary dead, unproductive. No matter how little, do everything in your capacity to realize your vision to fulfill your assignment and have your generation celebrate your good works.

My pastor has always said, "don't always wait for a perfect condition to take steps, rather perfect the conditions by taking steps." Each time he makes this statement, it gets me on my toes again, significantly if I have been delaying in taking steps in achieving a particular goal.

Friend, make that phone call now, visiting that prospect of yours now, or starting with that insufficient fund now. It might just be the action that will set your vision in motion. Obviously, you know it's only a car in motion that can get to its destination, and so also is it when you back your vision with action, will there be a realization.

Note! Lookers become an object for mockers. So take responsibility and take it now!

STEP 5: DEDICATION

I often describe an action as taking your seed to the field, and dedication, planting that seed into the soil. There is an extent to which action can take you to realize your vision without it been backed by dedication. I can also define dedication as a total commitment to the pursuit of every vision.

When you are committed to a course, you will have no reason to turn back no matter what, you are always ready to go on. I have not seen any meaningful achievement that does not require absolute dedication, as I have learned, "what you do not pay attention to will never grow."

In as much as growth is natural for every living being, some other factors also are responsible for growth, such as a balanced diet, exercise, proper medication, and so many other factors. Once you are not committed to your car's needs regularly, you will need one day soon to be grounded, just like many visionaries due to a lack of dedication to their God-given Vision. Staying at it till it works is what dedication is.

Never underestimate the power of dedication. It can turn small beginnings into great endings. Your absolute commitment to the little insignificant result you have now can turn it into a mind-blowing, trailblazing, and pace-setting achievement.

It is very accurate that sometimes the environment we find ourselves might be limiting us from forging ahead in the pursuit of our vision. Still, I can categorically tell you that as long as God gives the vision, your dedication to it will certainly turn things around. When demolishers want to bring down a building, they don't hit the building once. They hit the wall several times over till it collapses.

Your effort in fulfilling your vision must be repeatedly consistent. I call it persistence; every vision requires persistence; otherwise, you won't accomplish it.

Too many people get tired too soon; according to the Bible, there is no future for a lazy person. Nothing comes cheap, even salvation; the Bible says we should work out our salvation with fear and trembling. You must be prepared to work and stay working if you must turn your vision into reality.

You must be ready to give your total self to whatever you believe in; it will never work. In Mark 10: 28-30, one of Jesus' disciples made a remark saying, *"Master we have left all to follow your vision, what do we have to gain?"* Jesus replied, *"you will get a hundred percent fulfillment"* (paraphrased).

Let me conclude with this statement, "Vision is the seed of exploits & dedication is the planting of that seed."

STEP 6: CONFESSION

Words indeed are powerful, but when it is not confessed or spoken, it loses its potency, and so does every vision lose its potential of coming into reality when it is not back with a faith-filled confession. I have heard several times that the life of our future is in the mouth. Initially, I didn't understand until I read in the Bible where it says, "Death and life are in the power of the tongue, and those who love it will eat its fruit" (*see Proverb 18:21*).

Your WORDS has the power to either ignite the passion for believing and pursue the fulfillment of your vision or completely dowse the fire in you. Every vision pursued must be backed with positive confessions; otherwise, one may never see through it. What you believe in must be publicly declared not for the advertisement but to activate your faith.

In Mark 11: 23, Jesus Christ explains how the believer's confession is essential to activating faith to realize our God-given Vision. He said, "***Assuredly, I say to you, whoever says to this mountain be removed and be cast into the sea', and does not doubt in his heart, but believes that those things he says will be done, he will have whatever he says.***"

Jesus was simply saying that our confession initiates the manifestation of our God-given Vision. If no one can become a born-again Christian without confessing his/her faith in Jesus as Lord, this tells you how important and influential confession is to every believer. If God spoke creation into existence, and everything exists today was spoken into being by God (Genesis 1), you and I must master the art of faith-filled confessions.

The power of confession is underused in this current generation. Today, believers desire to see the reality of God's promises before they can declare it; unfortunately, kingdom dimensions don't function this way; your declaration is what brings it into manifestation. When God created light to lighten up the whole world according to Genesis 1; He didn't need to see the light in reality before He declared it.

According to Genesis 1:1-3, the entire earth was void and filled with darkness, but when God, who is Light stepped in, He declared, **"Let there be light"** and based on His confession 'there was light."

Do not wait for things to get better before you can confidently say it out; what you won't say, you may not see. It doesn't matter how ridiculous what God shows you may sound, refuse to allow the fear or ridicule stop you from confessing your desired outcome. Long before Jesus' became the way to our salvation, he had been saying it "I am the way, I am the way" even though many did not believe in Him'.

What is it that you have heard about your future that you have been afraid to say out or dream of becoming someone you have been nurturing but could not share with anyone? It is time to be bold enough to begin to make positive confessions about it, and you will find out that there is tremendous transformation power in positive confession.

Jesus Christ explains how it works in John chapter 6:63, saying, "…*the words that I speak to you are spirit, and they are life*." The words that we speak carry a spirit, and this spirit is a life-given spirit.

Don't be afraid of making a declaration of your vision, say what you believe in, and leave people to their opinion. Shame robs men of their fame!

Eight months before I released my first book, I started talking about my newly released book when I didn't even have any money to start the project. Still, I was not discouraged because I already knew the secrets of turning the invisible into the visible. Part of which is a positive confession, so I increased the tenacity I was saying. Also, maintaining a good and strong connection to God, with my unwavering commitment to the steps I shared in the previous chapters. Eventually, the book came out and silenced everyone who did not believe my confessions.

Friend, when you wake up in the morning, stand up and say to yourself, "this is what God has said concerning me, and that is what I will be" there is no devil that will stop you from becoming what God has told you that you will be. Change your negative confessions to positive ones and watch the trajectory of your life take a positive turn.

I remember telling my friends that I will get married very early in life. Some of my friends that heard me make such confession felt that my boasting was just too much because I had not even completed high school, and here was I already talking about marriage. The truth is that it happened at just the right time I wanted it, even though my condition then was not as colorful and bright as it is now, but I did. I make bold to say that after the gift of Christ, there isn't any other gift as precious as my darling wife, Busola" of 15 years.

Every confession made continuously in line with one's destiny brings you closer to its reality because the more you say it, the more you believe it, and the more you believe it, the easier it is for you to achieve it. Go ahead!

STEP 7: CELEBRATION

If you wonder what celebration has got to do with turning your vision into a reality, allow me to say "everything." Praising God in advance for what you haven't seen is a demonstration of absolute faith in God.

A powerful principle I have learned from well-accomplished men and women of faith. They say, when you celebrate your God-given Vision, you are also celebrating the giver of the vision, and that provokes his attention towards the fulfillment of your vision.

Celebrating God also means praising God, and when you praise God, He will surely raise you. Celebration leads to multiplication as Psalm 67:5 states, **"Let the people praise God, and the Lord will bless us; let the praise God, and then the earth will yield its increase."**

Praising God connects you to divine supply for the fulfillment of your God-given Vision. Also, praising God should be when things are working out fine; praise Him, even more, when things are not turning out as you planned. It is vital to have at the back of your mind that God will make way for you.

I have never seen any complainer who ends up achieving something great in life. Look at anyone who you know whose life is positive and worth emulating. You will notice that these set of people have got an appreciative lifestyle. Even when things are rough, you will never hear them murmur. Instead, they maintain a positive attitude, and that keeps them thanks to God.

It is the same way you tend to move closer to people who appreciate you that God moves closer to those who appreciate Him. It will be much easier for you to get something from a person who knows you appreciate him or her, likewise with God. Celebrating God will always attract you and supply directly from Him who gave you the assignment, no matter how much you will need for its accomplishment.

There is a man in the Bible whose addiction to this principle inspires me a lot; he always had God on his side all the time just because he never stops celebrating God. David had so many resources to fulfill any assignment God gave to him, such that even when he had privileges to get things done for free, he always insisted he will pay the cost (*See* 2 Samuel 24:24).

Every vision has a cost attached to it that must be paid in full, most times. You will need more than what you have, but there is one who has more than what you need to fulfill your assignment, and one of the very best ways you can gain access to His supplies is through praise.

I often said that "when you pray, God sends one of His ministering angels to attend to you, but when you praise, He comes down Himself." The Bible says God inhabits the praises of His people. In other words, when your vision is causing you to praise Him, God takes over your vision, and when He does, you can be rest assured that nothing can stop its fulfillment.

As I mentioned in the early chapters of this book, when God gave me the revelation of my first book, I did in line with fulfilling it to create a graphical illustration of the cover design. I remember that I deliberately wrote on it these words, "Thank You Lord For Its Reality," Then I glued it on the wall where I could see it every morning, day, and night to enable me to remember to keep thanking God for its reality. It worked! I published my book - ***The Seed-principle of fruitfulness***, and its impact traveled far and wide.

No one will help you appreciate your vision; in fact, people don't celebrate visions until you realize it. Regardless of what people are saying, get on your praise. Those who are mocking you today will eventually celebrate you because of what God will do in your life. In the time past, many have mocked me for pursuing God's plan for my life. Of course, some were painful, but that couldn't stop me from thanking God for each position I found myself. I discovered that the more I appreciated God, the more I appreciated in life. I once, a mentor of mine said, "If you don't thank God for your present meal, you may never have a change of menu." Each time I think about this statement, it motivates me to stay grateful no matter my current condition.

I don't know what level you are or what your vision is, at the moment, but I believe this is the right moment to say "thank you, Lord, thank you Lord for where I have been, where I am right now, and where I am going to be."

Get on it now, because it works!

STEP 8: EXPECTATION

This chapter is the last step you are required to take to give birth to your vision. Just as you know that no woman enters into the delivery room without expecting a baby, so will you not be able to give birth to your vision without an expectation of it coming into reality.

The delivery of your vision is at the mercy of your expectation because only what you expect has a right to happen to you. Nothing that you are not expecting will ever come your way; with God, nothing happens suddenly; it must be that it is wanted.

Today, everything that happens to me results from my expectations, either good or bad, consciously, or subconsciously. The realization of your vision requires the backing of your expectation; the level of your expectancy will determine the speed of delivery. There is excellent power imbedded in expectation. It's so powerful that it commands a reality of its focused object. I never expected anything short of the result I am getting now because I remained optimistic even in the uncertain times of obvious deprivation. My first book's success is almost no surprise because my expectations were very high, and I was not afraid to talk about it to anyone who cared to listen.

The question is, what are you expecting out of your life while in school or now in your career? I am asking you this question because many young men and women have failed in answering this very question. Every opportunity I have during counseling sessions with a young adult, I asked them, "what are you expecting?" 80% of them can not say what they expect in their pursuit and, even worse, no aspiration. Some are running because others are running, not because there is an expected end to the race.

Let there be something beautiful in your mind that you expect to happen to you even though your environment is not beautiful. Your environment is essential in fulfilling your vision but not as needed as your mind's environment because your inner world controls your outer world.

In Proverbs 23:18, the Bible says, **_"For surely there is an end, and your expectation shall not be cut off."_**

It means that there is fulfillment for every vision received from God, but your expectation is a primary key for seeing the end of your pursuit in life. Without the key to expectation, the door of fulfillment will remain close.

As I conclude on this note, allow me to suggest that you never let a day pass by without you having a positive expectation concerning your day and your vision in life. Great miracles are products of great expectations.

Don't let the situations of today blind you from seeing the possibilities of tomorrow.

So, reactivate your hope and expect something much better, because expectation works, it's the key to manifestation.

Welcome to a new level in Jesus' name, Amen!

THE FINAL WORD:
GRACE IN FULFILLING YOUR VISION

"By the grace of God, I am What I am, and His grace towards me was not in vain; but I labored more abundantly than they all, yet not I, but the grace of God which was with me." – 1 Corinthians 15:10

I want to share that it will set you apart in the race of accomplishing your life assignment; it will determine how colorful and bright your vision will appear when fulfilled. You will indeed have to pay the price to achieve greatness in life, but you can also pay it gracefully, such that you might not even know you are paying any cost.

The Lord said to me early in the year 2006, He said to me in these words, "Femi, many young men and women are trying to fulfill My purpose for their lives with certificates, qualification and recommendation and that is why they are struggling. Go! Teach them the word of grace, bringing them into the reality of my blessing, telling them no man can enjoy true fulfillment in life except My Grace is present in their pursuit.

There is less stress on a bolted joint when it is well greased. So also, will you not need much strength with the grace of God. Grace makes your journey more comfortable. What took others one year by grace will cost you six months. Apart from diligence, the speed and blessing I am enjoying today in my life, ministry, family, and business result from the Grace of God.

Grace is the; G-gift of God R-received from A-above to C-create E-exploits.

Without the gift of God, no one can do exploits in life, it requires something out of the ordinary to do extraordinary things, and that is what the gift of grace does; with the gift of grace, you are a supernaturally empowered on earth!

No honest great man or woman will tell you that it was all by their ability that they achieved greatness in life; no one can do it by himself/herself. For our life to be glorious, we need the Grace of God, which also can be called God's favor, and favor is superior to luck.

No matter how bad the situation has been for you, the Grace of God is sufficient to convert the situation into something you will live to celebrate for the rest of your life, just as I am doing today. Grace is the only thing that makes failure worth celebrating because it doesn't work in perfect conditions.

Grace is for those who acknowledge their insufficiency, inadequacy, and weakness before God. They come to God entirely depending on Him and not on their strength or their knowledge.

Despite the unfathomable knowledge, wisdom, understanding, and skill Jesus Christ had, yet the Bible still says about Him that "*He was full of grace*" (John 1:14). Everyone who wants to maximize his or her destiny should embrace the Grace of God. If he needed it, to fulfill His assignment, you and I need it, without a measure.

Apostle Paul in the book first Corinthians 15:10, said, "*By the grace 'of God I am what I am, and His grace toward me was not in vain, but I labored more abundantly than they all, yet not I, but the grace of God which was with me.*"

As a child of God, if God's Grace doesn't back your hard work, you will struggle. You can't succeed the way God designed for you to succeed. You don't have to sweat to prosper; there are people I know today whose success has nothing to do with sweat but by diligence and ultimately, God's Grace at work in them.

The Grace of God must back every principle that governs vision dynamics because any race without grace ends in disgrace. Someone said it is the absence of grace that is called a disgrace.

If you don't want to end up in disgrace in your pursuit of the vision, you need to be more conscious of God's grace available to all who want it. One of the fastest ways to get the Grace of God to work on your life is service, serving God and humanity. Every real vision is about service; no vision is about the visionary; it's about people. Any vision that is not people-oriented is not a vision from God. What the Bible says is **"*where there is no vision the people perish*.** "Vision has been about people; it is still about people, and it will forever be about people.

I have been doing nothing in my past that my focus has not been about blessing people because one-way grace can multiply in my life. Sometimes ago, I got invited to speak at a conference, and I was to speak on the subject 'My testimony of service". And I asked myself if I had only one sentence to express myself, what would I say? So, I began to think deeply, and finally, I arrived at what I could point out as my testimony of service, which is the Grace of God.

The Grace of God has made all the difference in my life today because some great things have happened to me, and I know very well that this has nothing to do with my ability or my certificate. As an end to this last chapter, it is with one the most powerful statement of the Bible recorded in the book of Ephesians 2:8 *"**For by grace you have been saved through faith, and that not of yourselves; it is the gift of God.**"*

I pray for you to receive yours now in the name of Jesus, amen!

SCRIPTURE MEDITATION ON VISION

"I will stand my watch And set myself on the rampart, And watch to see what He will say to me, And what I will answer when I am corrected. Then the LORD answered me and said: "Write the vision And make it plain on tablets, That he may run who reads it. For the vision is yet for an appointed time; But at the end it will speak, and it will not lie. Though it tarries, wait for it; Because it will surely come, It will not tarry." Habakkuk2:1-3NKJV

"Then the word of the LORD came to me, saying: "Before I formed you in the womb I knew you; Before you were born I sanctified you; I ordained you a prophet to the nations." Then said I: "Ah, Lord GOD! Behold, I cannot speak, for I am a youth." But the LORD said to me: "Do not say, 'I am a youth,' For you shall go to all to whom I send you, And whatever I command you, you shall speak. Do not be afraid of their faces, For I am with you to deliver you," says the LORD. Then the LORD put forth His hand and touched my mouth, and the LORD said to me: "Behold, I have put My words in your mouth. See, I have this day set you over the nations and over the kingdoms, To root out and to pull down, To destroy and to throw down, To build and to plant." Moreover the word of the LORD came to me, saying, "Jeremiah, what do you see?" And I said, "I see a branch of an almond tree." Then the LORD said to me, "You have seen well, for I am ready to perform My word.""Jeremiah1:4-12NKJV

"Then God said, "Let Us make man in Our image, according to Our likeness; let them have dominion over the fish of the sea, over the birds of the air, and over the cattle, over all the earth and over every creeping thing that creeps on the earth." So God created man in His own image; in the image of God He created him; male and female He created them. Then God blessed them, and God said to them, "Be fruitful and multiply; fill the earth and subdue it; have dominion over the fish of the sea, over the birds of the air, and over every living thing that moves on the earth.""Genesis1:26-28NKJV

"Moreover whom He predestined, these He also called; whom He called, these He also justified; and whom He justified, these He also glorified."Romans8:30NKJV

"Where there is no prophetic vision the people cast off restraint, but blessed is he who keeps the law." Proverbs29:18ESV

"For I know the thoughts that I think toward you, says the LORD, thoughts of peace and not of evil, to give you a future and a hope."Jeremiah29:11NKJV

Notes

Notes

Notes

Notes

Notes

Notes

Notes

Notes

Notes

Notes

Notes

Notes

Notes

Notes

Notes

Notes